The Land of AMPERSAND

Where Imagination Runs Wild

Cynthia Correll

Jump For Joy Press

Saint Louis, Missouri

The Land of Ampersand
Where Imagination Runs Wild

Cynthia Correll
Jump For Joy Press

Published by Jump For Joy Press, St. Louis, MO

Interior design: Davis Creative, DavisCreative.com

Library of Congress Cataloging-in-Publication Data
Library of Congress Control Number: 2021919702

Publisher's Cataloging-In-Publication Data
(Prepared by The Donohue Group, Inc.)

Names: Correll, Cynthia, author, artist.
Title: The Land of Ampersand : where imagination runs wild / Cynthia Correll.
Description: Saint Louis, Missouri : Jump For Joy Press, (2021)
Identifiers: ISBN 9781737887607
Subjects: LCSH: Ampersand--Pictorial works. | Printing--Pictorial works. | Imagination--Pictorial works. | LCGFT: Illustrated works. | BISAC: SELF-HELP / Personal Growth / Happiness. | DESIGN / Graphic Arts / Typography. | HUMOR / Form / Pictorial.
Classification: LCC Z111 .C67 2021 | DDC 686.21--dc23

2021

For anyone who is curious

ampersand • *\am-pər-sand* • *noun:*
a character "&" that is used for the word "and"

Merriam-Webster

Your Self-Guided Tour Begins Here...

As you enter *The Land of Ampersand*, get ready for a rejuvenating journey through a world of positivity and playfulness. Notice the inhabitants are as welcoming as they are amusing! Renowned for their freedom of expression, they invite you to linger and delight. In this curious environment, you can leave your worries behind, immerse yourself in the realm of possibility, and let your imagination run wild.

Right now, you might be wondering about the origin of the Ampersands. Their history dates back to Roman times when the spoken phrase "and per se and" was shortened to "and." The written abbreviation became a combination of the letters "et"—giving birth to the curvaceous and elegant Ampersand symbols. Over the past centuries, the DNA of the Ampersands evolved into an inventive and celebrated dynasty of characters—thanks to creative typeface artists around the globe.

Thank you for visiting *The Land of Ampersand*, famous for its hospitality and enchantment. We hope you enjoy your adventure. Feel free to browse chronologically from beginning to end—or drop in anywhere you like. Let your fingers meander at your own pace through the whimsical landscape.

The Ampersand descendants are best known for unifying all things and allowing opposites to co-exist. As you travel on your self-guided tour, remember to breathe, relax, and savor the promise of possibility.

*When you change the way
you look at things,
the things you look at change.*

Wayne Dyer

Feisty Ampersand,
more than just a pretty face

When Ampersands fly

Ampersand Masquerade

Who let the dog out?

Blushing Ampersand

Make waves,
not war

Ampersand Popsicle

Luck of the Ampersand

Through the
Ampersand Looking Glass

Where pearls & Ampersands
come from...

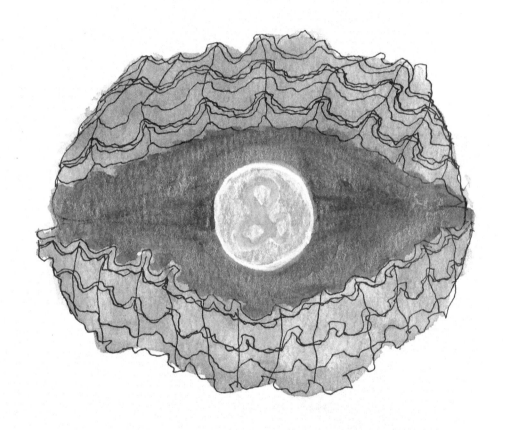

Fiddlehead Fern

Let there be light!

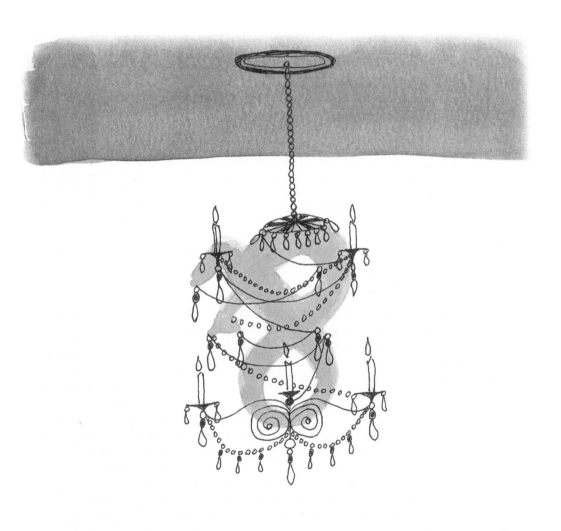

Ampersand Lost

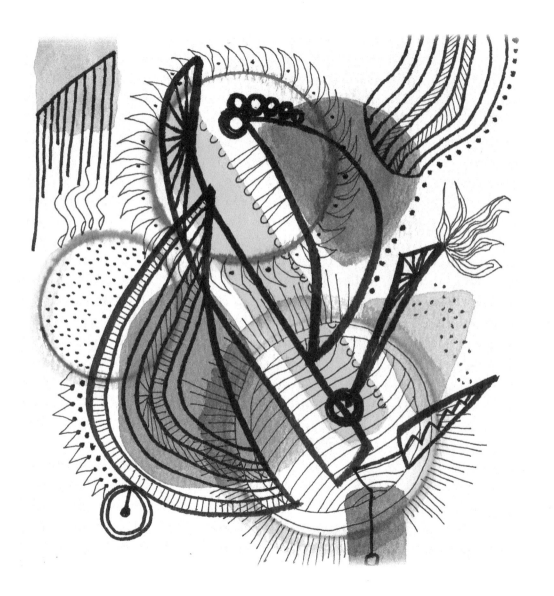

Spring has sprung!

The Spinning Ampersands
now performing

A Tree Grows
in Ampersand

Ampersand Relief Map

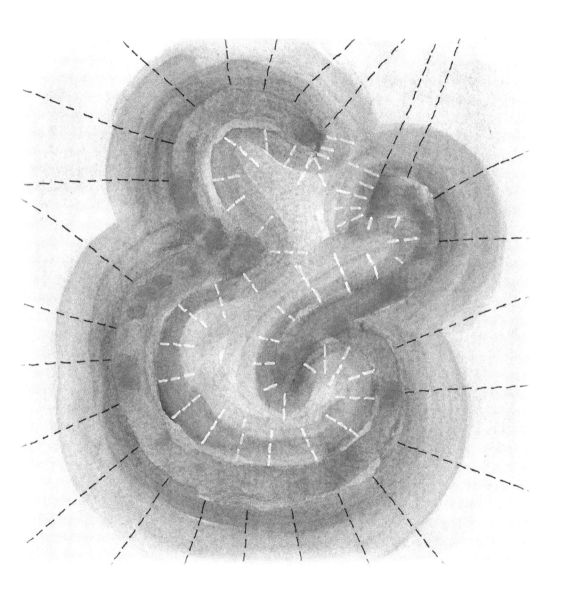

Ancestral Portrait

Object of the game

Ampersand
Infrastructure

Bouquet of
Ampersands

Crazy Ampersand Circus

Ampersand Window

Stay tuned
for Ampersand

Ampersand Who?

Her Royal
Ampersand Highness

Ampersand of the Tropics

Aced it!

Psychedelic
Ampersand

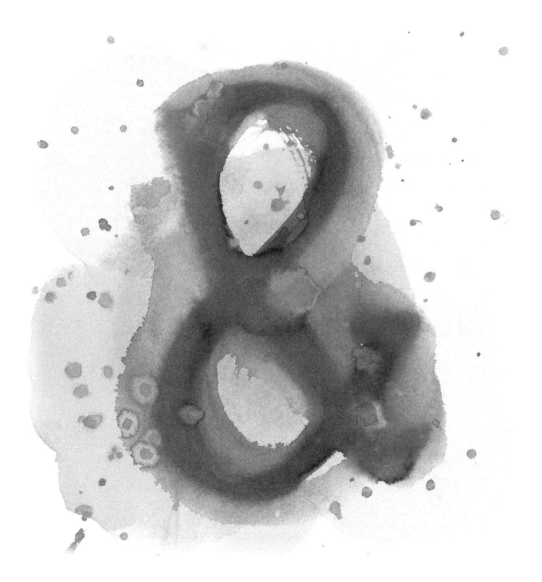

Royal Order
of Ampersand

Ampersand Stampede

Ampersand meets
the Equinox

Ampersand Paisley

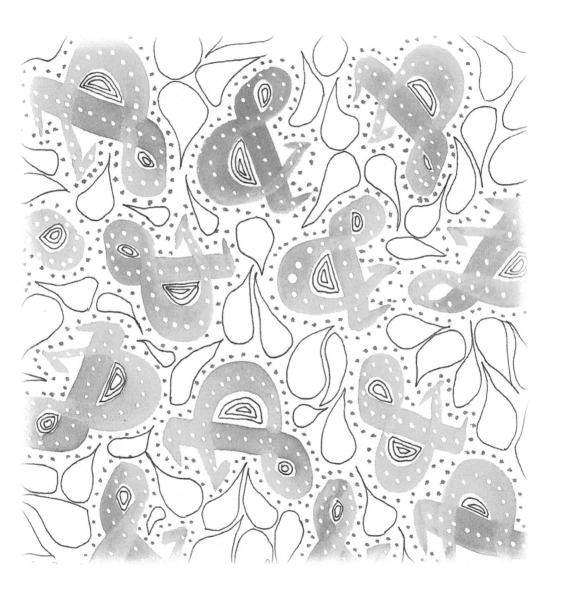

Got Ampersands
on a cloudy day!

Ampersand now serving

Tie-dye Magic

And many more!

Beyond Par

Effervescent
Ampersand

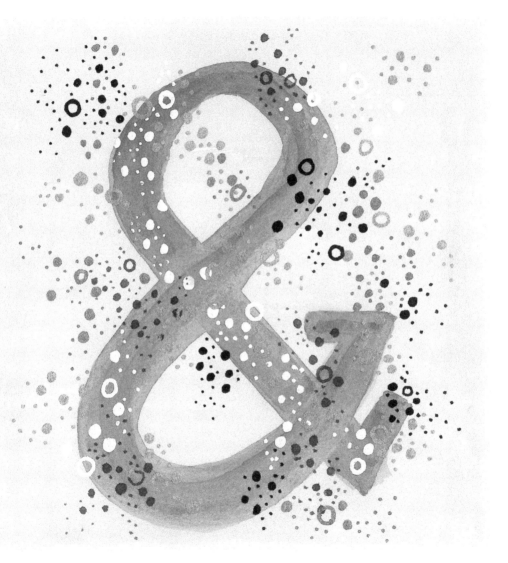

Charlotte's
Ampersand

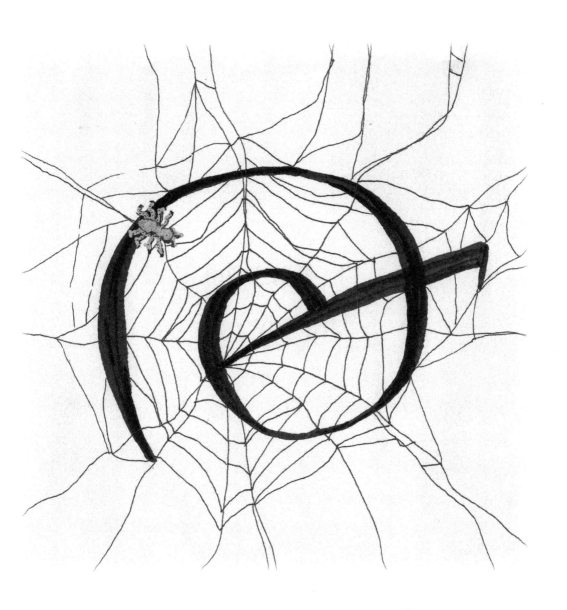

I'm too prickly
for my pot

Ampersand Pinball

This little
Ampersand piggy

Vintage Ampersand

Ampersand
for the birds

Sealed with an
Ampersand

Botanical
Ampersand

Miss Ampersand Beehive

The Ampersand
Naturalist

Fireworks Spectacular

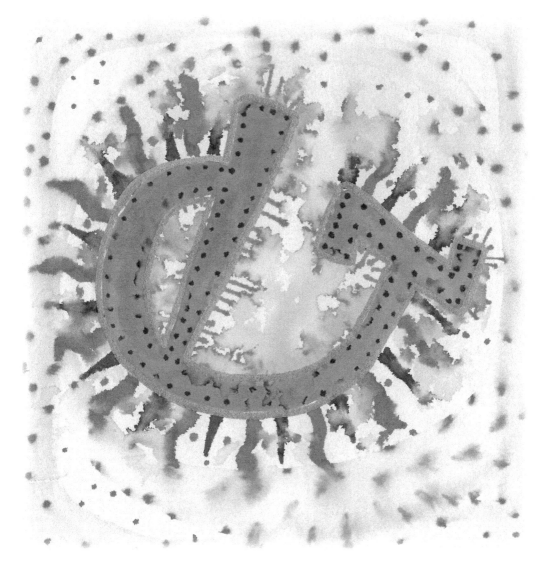

Seeing clearly now

      E   1

    F   **P**   2

  T   **O**   **Z**   3

 L **P** **E** **D**   4

P   E   C   F   D   5

E D F   C Z P   6

F E L O P Z D   7

L E F O D P C T   8

Ampersand Sea Urchin

Jewel of Ampersand

Cures-All

We are the champions!

Shadow play

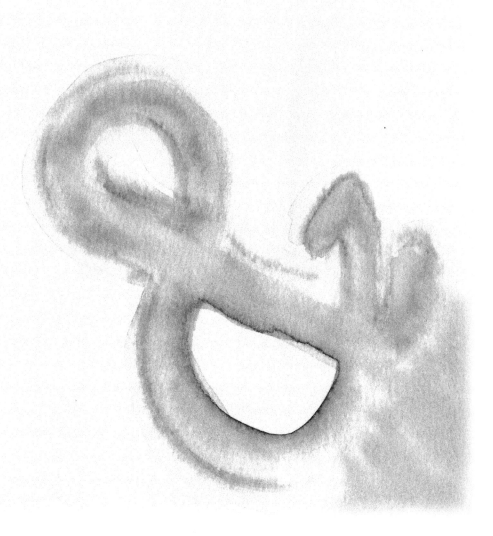

Together

What's new pussycat?

Ampersand Current

Happy trails!
Until we meet again...

*The real voyage of discovery consists not
in seeking new landscapes,
but in having new eyes.*

Marcel Proust

Your Turn for Ampersand Watching

Now it's your opportunity to engage in the timeless sport of Ampersand Watching. With a bit of quiet and patience, it's easy to catch an Ampersand in action.

When you spot one in your mind's eye, you are invited to record it here. Let your imagination run wild! No previous experience necessary. Just grab a pencil, paint brush or pen and begin!

Beyond The Land of Ampersand

Congratulations on completing your self-guided tour of *The Land of Ampersand*! You are officially awarded a Lifetime Ticket for you, your family, and your friends, to visit and revisit whenever you like.

As you return to reality, be sure to take your new perspective with you. Just as the rules of Improv Theatre remind us, we can respond with "yes, and" instead of "but"—unlocking fresh ideas and new opportunities. Going forward, please continue to experience and share the feelings of inclusion and positivity and joy!

Look around and notice how opposites attract, connections expand, and possibilities arise. Take time to immerse yourself again and again in this playful ritual of renewal at *The Land of Ampersand*.

Appreciation

I am immeasurably grateful to my precious family and my beloved friends who buoyed me in my quest for *The Land of Ampersand*. Thank you for believing in my expedition and cheering me on!

Cynthia Correll is an award-winning mixed-media artist and a creative entrepreneur, known as the Communication Architect. In her thought-provoking and whimsical work, she combines art, logic and structure to inspire and entertain the viewer. By generating more harmony and joy in the world, she hopes to motivate social reform. Cynthia naturally looks to the future, confronting traditional ideas by tapping into her instinct for embracing change and seeing possibilities. As a visual artist, she has exhibited around the country. One show favorite was her mason jar filled with alphabet soup and labeled "*The Complete Works of Wm. Shakespeare – Shake Before Reading*"

www.cynthiacorrell.com,

Instagram: cynthiacorrell

CPSIA information can be obtained
at www.ICGtesting.com
Printed in the USA
BVHW061038291121
622783BV00014B/359

9 781737 887607